Gammy

A Story about Alzheimer's Disease

Seneca Monique

Copyright © 2020 Seneca Monique
All rights reserved
First Edition

Fulton Books, Inc.
Meadville, PA

Published by Fulton Books 2020

ISBN 978-1-64654-540-7 (paperback)
ISBN 978-1-64654-541-4 (digital)

Printed in the United States of America

This book is dedicated to my husband, Jason. Thank you for supporting me through this process. I love you immensely. To my daughters Kerrington (Kerri) and Makenzi, you absolutely are the best girls a momma could ask for and I love you so much. To my son, JJ, thank you for the gift of you. I prayed for a son for a long time. Lastly, to my mom (Darnetta) and the Ridley family, you guys have been the best cheerleaders ever. There is not a family on this earth that loves the way that we do. Lets keep the energy and the rhythm forever flowing. Thank you!

1

Eight-year-old Carrie rushed about her room, searching for her socks and shoes. It was almost time to go and see Gammy! Her tummy began to rumble as she thought about Gammy's homemade triple chocolate chip cookies, soft and warm from the oven and drizzled with gooey caramel! She and Gammy would bake them together every time she visited.

"I have the best cookie-making Gammy in the world!" Carrie said to herself. "No, the universe! That's bigger!"

Carrie and Gammy also loved to read books and learn new words. Carrie loved to try them out on her mother and her friends.

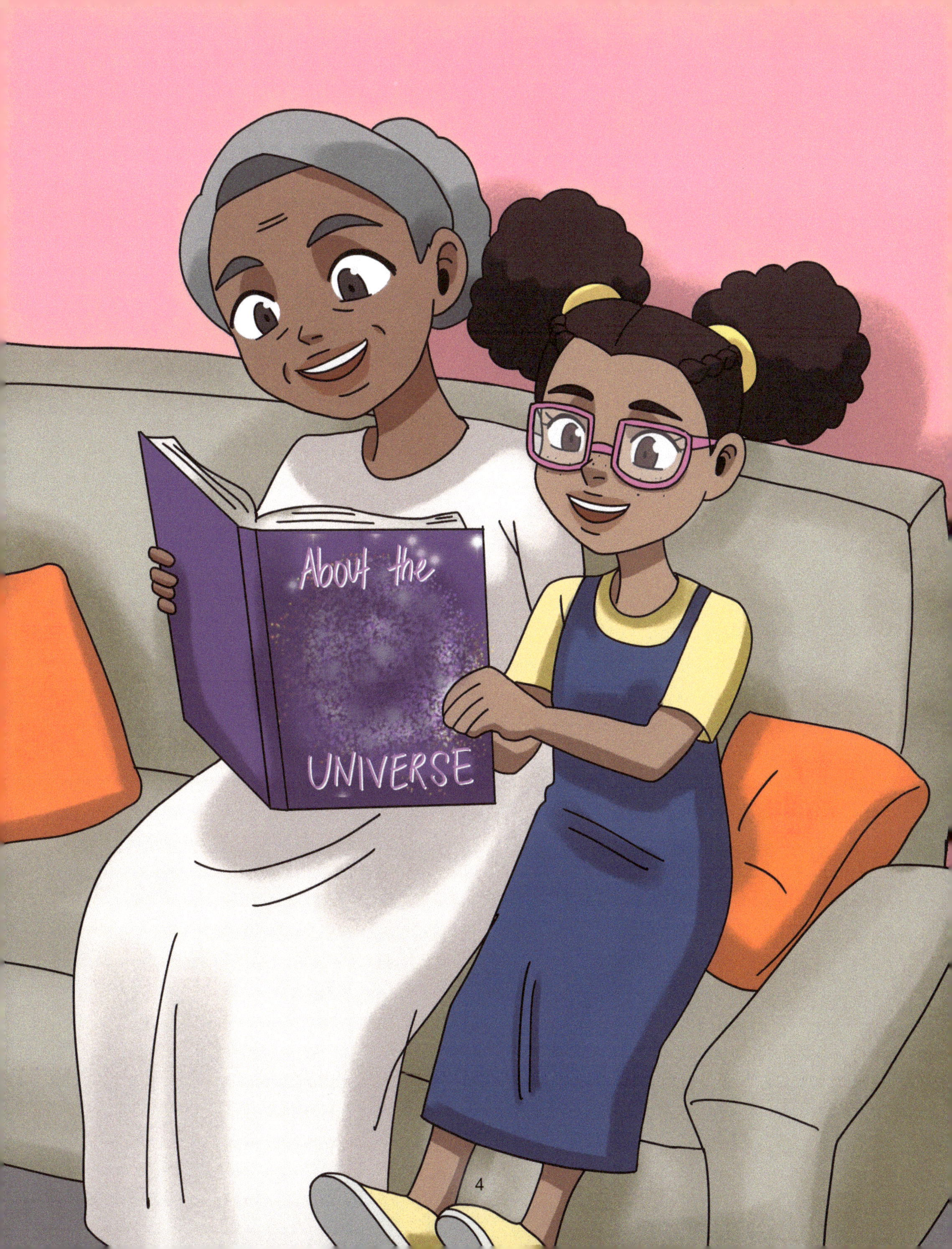
About the
UNIVERSE

In the car on the way to Gammy's, Carrie's mother was quiet. Soon, they pulled up in front of a strange building.

"This isn't Gammy's house," Carrie said.

"No, Carrie, it isn't," her mother replied. "We need to talk."

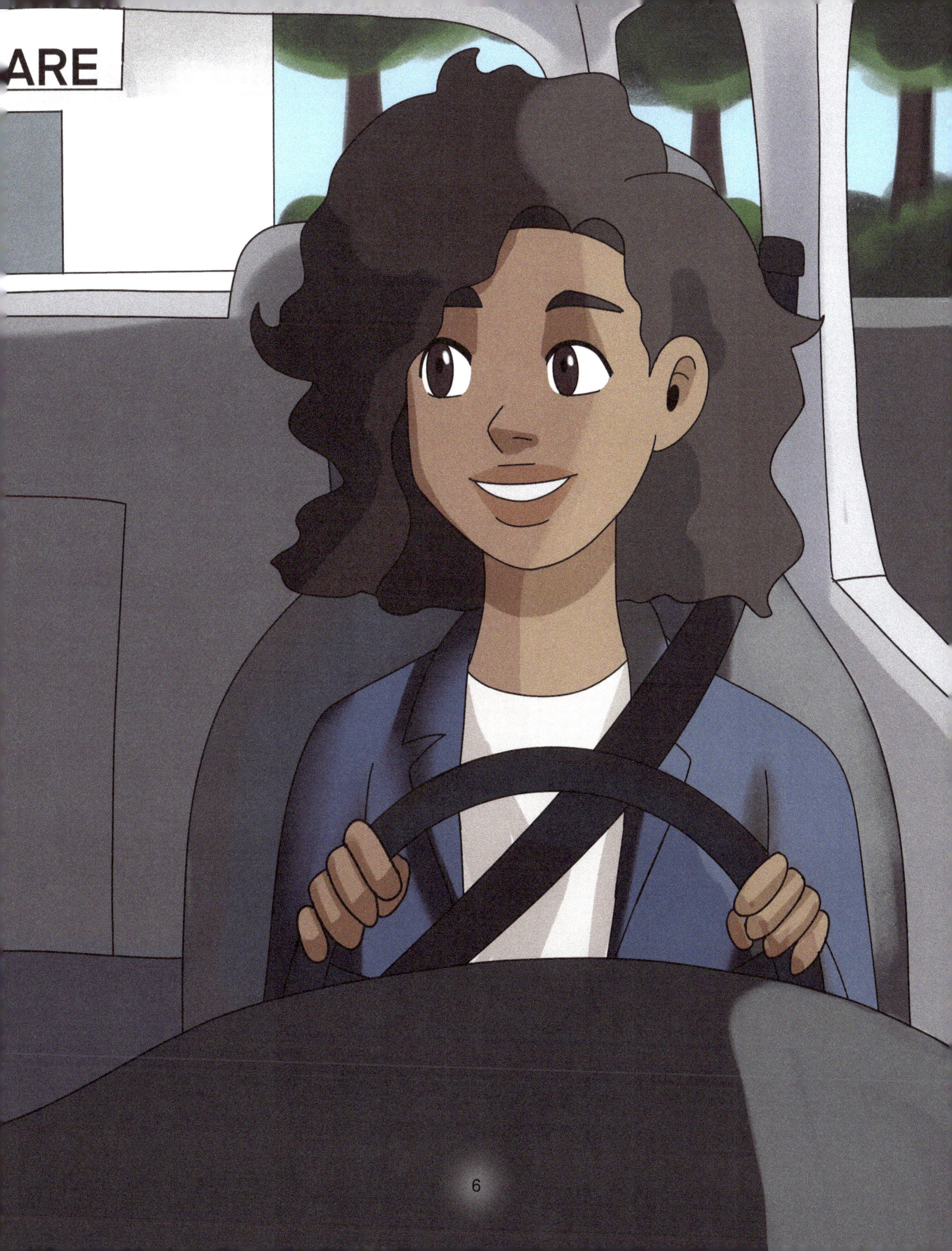
ARE

They got out of the car, and her mother led her over to a bench. They sat down. "Why aren't we going to Gammy's?" Carrie asked.

"We are at Gammy's, Carrie. This place is her new home," her mother said.

Carrie frowned as she looked around her. There were lots of older people outside on the lawn, some in wheelchairs, some walking with canes, others being helped along by nurses.

Carrie shook her head. "I don't understand."

"Awhile ago," her mother said, "Gammy accidentally started a fire in her house. She can't live by herself anymore. She has a disease called Alzheimer's. She must live here now, where she will be safe and people can care for her."

"What's Al…Alz—"

"Alzheimer's," her mother repeated. "It's a disease that some people get, usually when they are very old but sometimes not, where they lose their memories and forget how to do things like cook or dress themselves. In time, they can forget who their loved ones are."

Carrie's eyes grew wide. "But Gammy would never forget me! I am her favorite! I am going to read one of my chapter books to her today, and I'm going to show her how I'm learning to write in cursive, and we are going to learn new words together and bake cookies, and—"

Her mother put her hand on Carrie's head and smoothed her hair. "Let's just go inside and see how she is doing, okay? Maybe you can read to her."

MEMORY CARE

As they walked inside the big building—*no, it's gigantic! That's bigger*, Carrie thought—it sort of looked like a hospital. She had been to one once when she had her tonsils taken out. She saw a sign that said, "Memory Care."

I hope they can take care of Gammy's memory so that she never forgets me, Carrie thought.

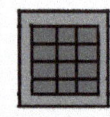

They came to a door, and her mother punched keys with large numbers on them. The door opened.

"Why can't we just open the door?" Carrie asked.

"It's for Gammy's safety," her mother said, "so she cannot wander about or get lost."

They walked down a long hallway with lots of doors. Carrie heard shouting, like someone was upset. It sounded like Gammy!

She and her mother entered a room that was painted a sunny yellow color. Gammy was seated in a rocking chair by the window.

A nurse stood nearby, holding a clipboard, and Gammy was wagging her finger and shouting, "You stole my money! You stole my money!"

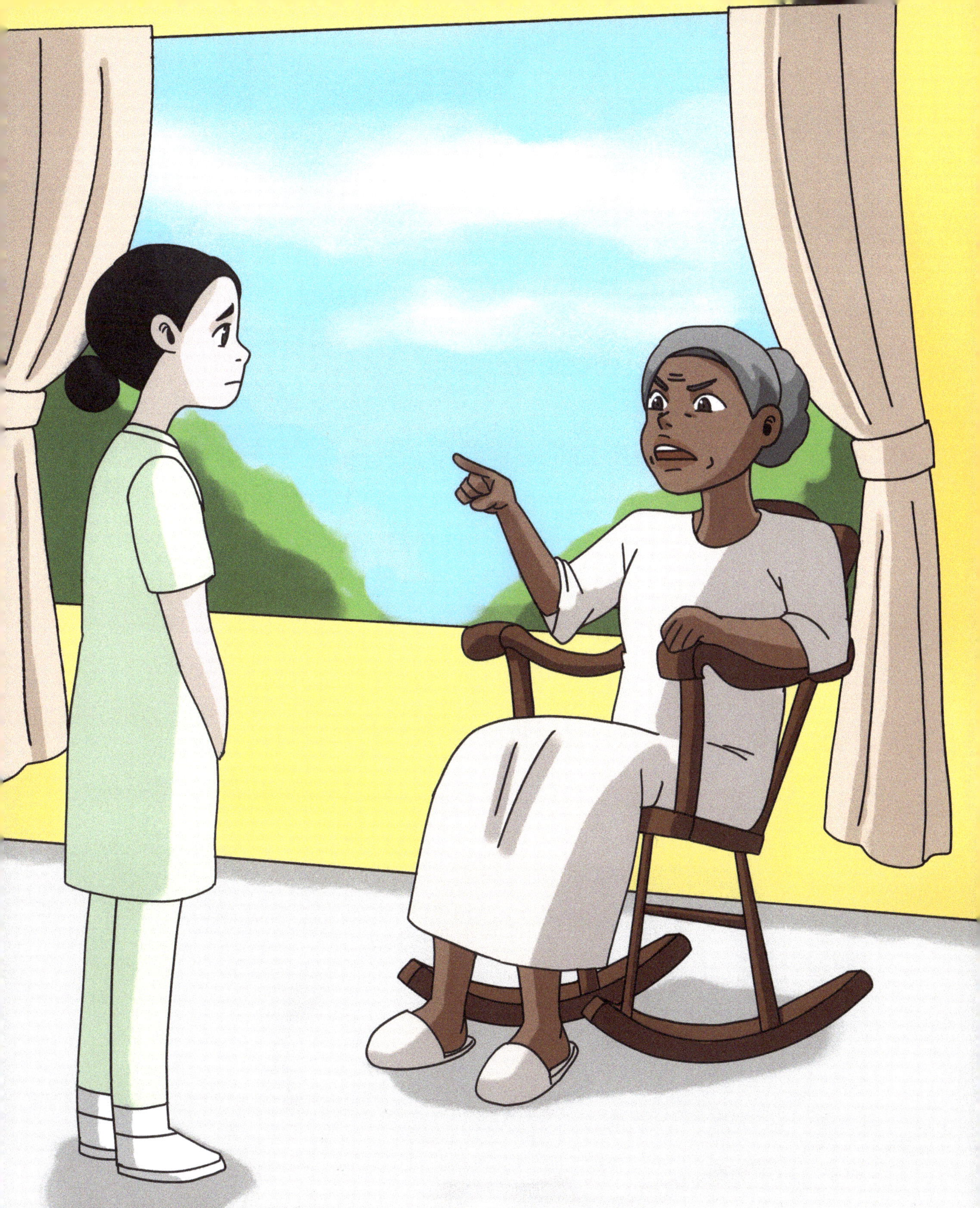

Carrie's mother rushed over and took Gammy's hand. "It's okay, Gammy. No one has stolen anything. Everything is fine. Look! Carrie is here to see you!"

Gammy suddenly began to cry.

Carrie rushed over and hugged her. "Don't be sad, Gammy! I am here, and I am so glad—no, I'm enthusiastic to see you! Remember when we learned that word?" Carrie began to cry too.

She and her mother stayed for a little while. Her mother talked softly to Gammy, and Carrie gave her lots of hugs. Soon the nurse gave Gammy some medicine, and it was time for her nap.

On the way home in the car, Carrie stared out the window and thought about all her wonderful memories with Gammy, like the times she helped her with her garden. They would go to the garden store and get big bags of black stinky dirt or soil. Gammy called it organic compost, but Carrie would hold her nose and say, "It just smells like poop to me!"

16

17

Gammy would just laugh. "It may smell bad," she would say, "but it grows the best veggies!"

And Gammy was right: every summer the garden would be full of flavorful vegetables! Carrie thought of freshly picked green tomatoes marinated in apple cider vinegar and fried with magical seasonings.

They were so tasty—no, they were scrumptious!

Later that night, after Carrie put on her favorite pajamas, her mother came into her room.

"I'm sorry you had to see Gammy when she wasn't feeling well. Do you have any questions?" she asked.

Carrie crawled up on her bed and sighed. "Does Alzheimer's disease make people forget how to be kind to others? Gammy always told me to be kind."

"It can sometimes have that effect on people," her mother replied. "Gammy's brain is sort of, well, broken now. It's not working the way it used to. Imagine if you woke up one day and everything and everyone you knew were now strange and unfamiliar. Imagine not remembering your favorite food, or your best friend's name, or that Brownie, your guinea pig, likes carrots at night. Gammy is still Gammy, but she gets confused and frustrated trying to remember things about her life. We have to be patient and show her that we love her and understand."

"But what if she can't even remember my name?" Carrie asked.

"Don't worry about that, Carrie. You just keep reading her stories, sharing things from school, and giving her lots of hugs, just as you always have. And always keep her in your prayers."

Her mother kissed her good night and left the room. Carrie got out of bed and got a sheet of paper and a pencil from her backpack. She began to write:

Gammy, it's me, Carrie, your granddaughter. I don't know if you know or not—I'm writing this poem for you, to help you remember what you forgot:

You are the best cook in the world—no, wait, make that the universe. You love to read, write, dance, laugh, and you never swear or curse.

You do not like peas or beets, so do not allow them on your plate.

You like to take walks outside in the sun to digest what you've just ate.

Gammy, your favorite color is neon green. We decided we liked that color together!

You love pandas, rainbows, and cowboy boots: the old black ones, made from rattlesnake leather.

When you think you know, but the thought just isn't clear, just remember that I love you and family is near.

You are my very best friend, my sunshine after it rains. You always make me feel better when I am in pain.

Now I will be your sunshine when the showers drown out your memories.

I will remind you of the adventures of Gammy and Carrie through poems and stories.

I love you, Gammy.

Love,
Carrie!

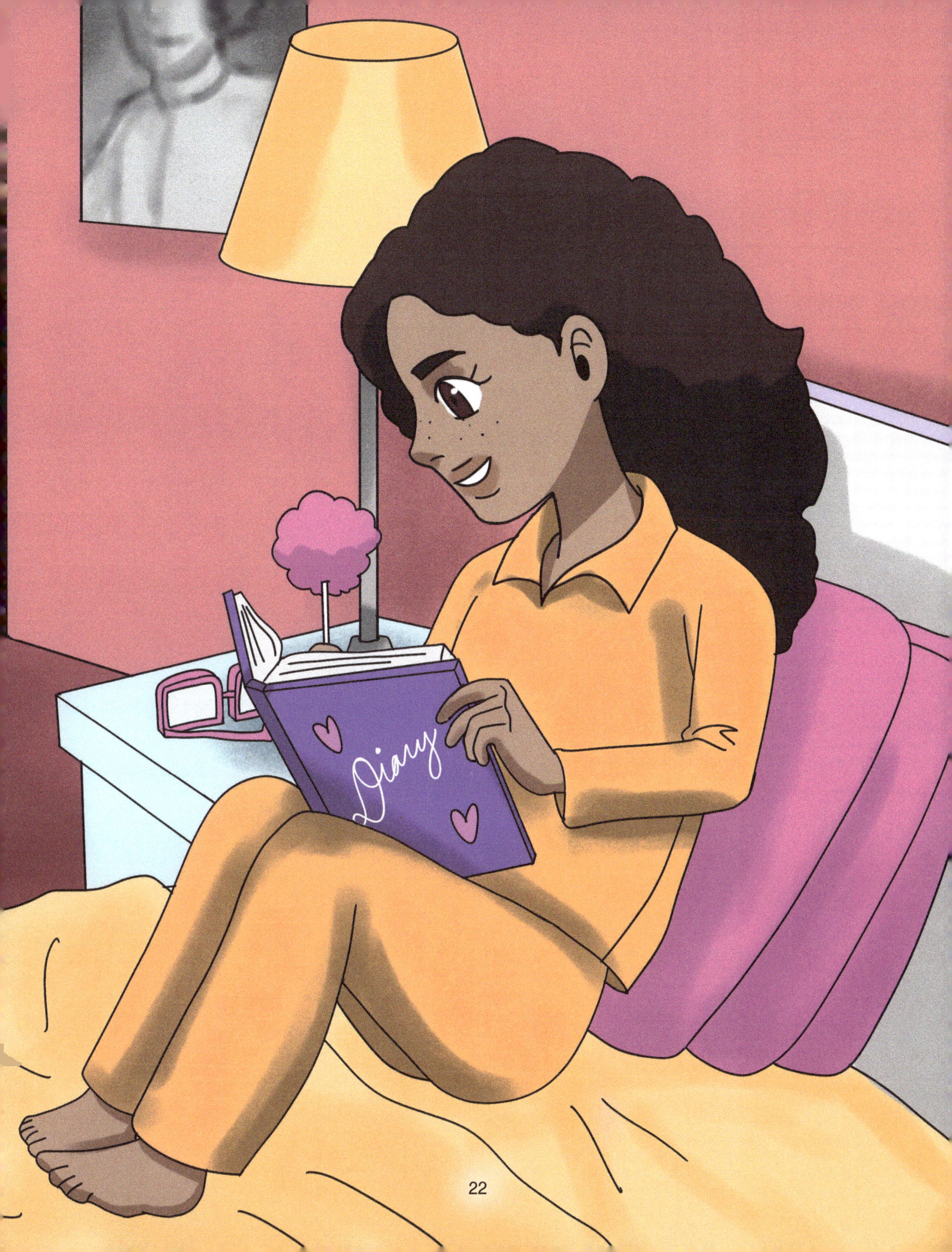
Diary

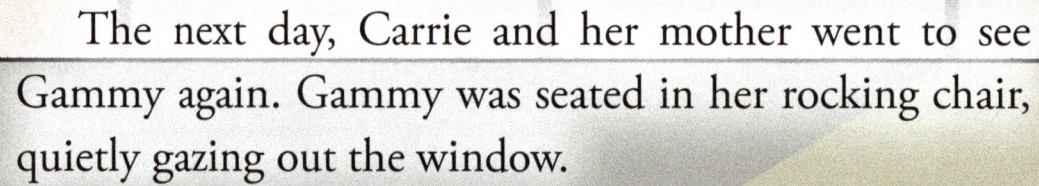

The next day, Carrie and her mother went to see Gammy again. Gammy was seated in her rocking chair, quietly gazing out the window.

When she turned to look at them, Carrie ran over and gave her a big—no, a colossal hug!

Carrie took out the poem she had written the night before and read it to Gammy. When she finished, she asked, "Did you like it, Gammy?"

Gammy just stared at her for a moment and then looked out the window once more.

Carrie was sad, but she reminded herself that Gammy's brain was broken but that, in her heart, Gammy still loved her. She walked over to a small bulletin board on the wall and reached for a tack to hang up the poem.

When Carrie turned around, Gammy mumbled, "I really like it when you read to me—no, *I love* it when you read to me!"

Carrie smiled and gave Gammy the biggest, most gigantic, most colossal hug ever. "You will always be my Gammy!"

The End

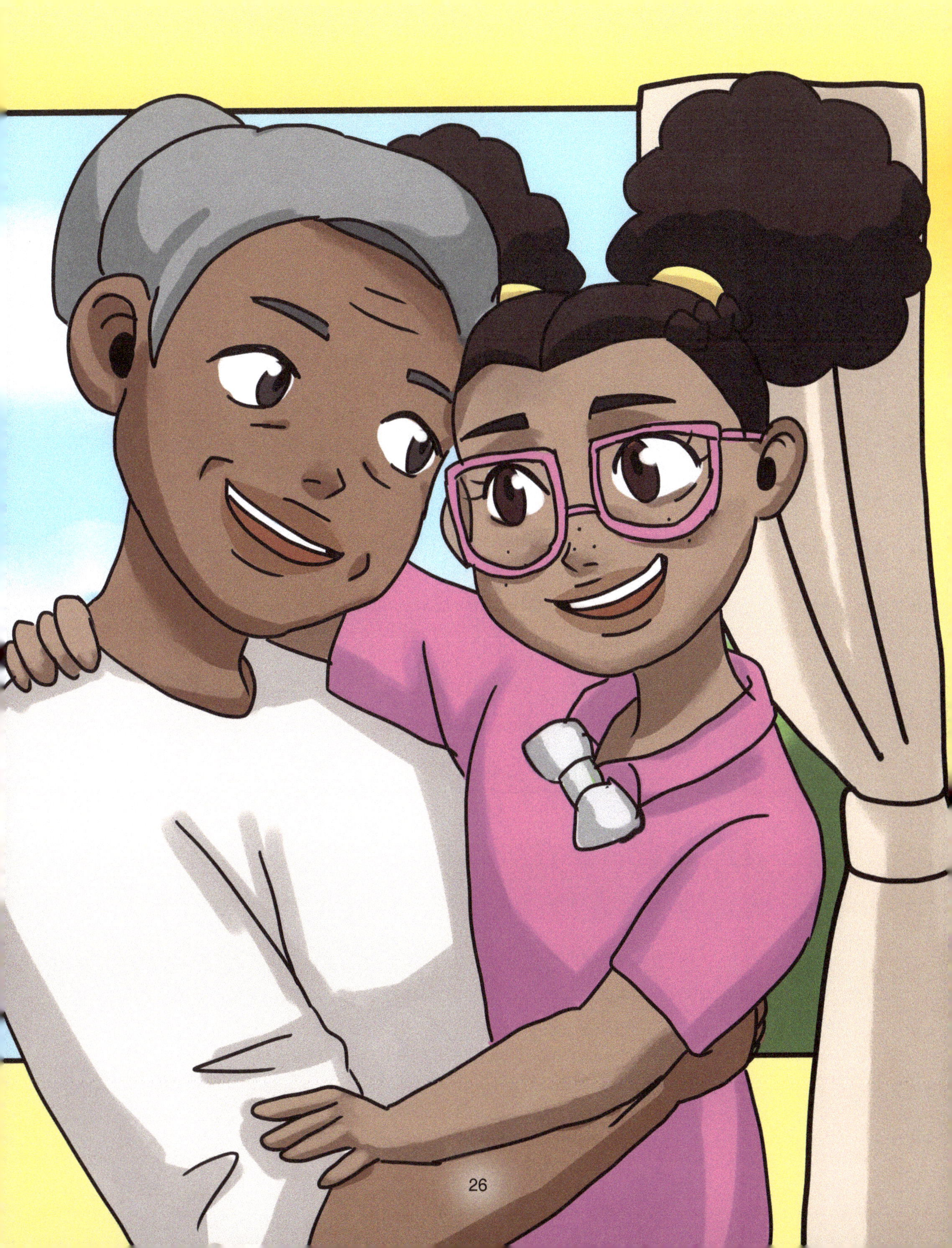

Hello there! Can you join Carrie in her quest to expand her vocabulary by remembering the meanings of these words?

        Enthusiastic
        Gigantic
        Scrumptious
        Universe
        Colossal

About the Author

Seneca is a graduate of Iona College in New York, where she holds a BA degree in English literature. She also has a masters of education degree from Northcentral University in Arizona. She is a proud wife and a mother. She has worn a plethora of hats throughout her career but is most passionate about serving her community and making sure little ones who are considered disadvantaged have the opportunity and the resources to shine and be their greatest self.